DIVORCE
RECOVERY

DIVORCE RECOVERY

DAVID A. SMART

Rapha Publishing/Word, Inc.

Houston and Dallas, TX

Divorce Recovery

by David A. Smart

Copyright © Rapha Publishing/Word, Inc.,
1991, Houston and Dallas, TX.

Unless otherwise indicated, scripture
quotations are based on the NEW
AMERICAN STANDARD BIBLE,
copyright © The Lockman Foundation,
1960, 1962, 1963, 1968, 1971, 1972, 1973,
1975, 1977. Those indicated NIV are from
The New International Version, copyright ©
1983 by International Bible Society,
Zondervan Bible Publishers.

First Printing, 1991
ISBN: 0-945276-36-2
Printed in the United States of America

CONTENTS

SCENES OF PAIN AND OPPORTUNITY 1

PERSONAL HEALING AND RECOVERY 9

GRIEVING: HURT, ANGER,
    AND FORGIVENESS 31

PRIMARY RELATIONSHIPS 41

CONCLUSION 69

INTRODUCTION

This booklet is intended as a source of hope, challenge, and recovery for persons whose marriages have ended in divorce.

It is assumed that a considerable degree of "hardness of heart" (Mark 10:5) existed on the part of one or both spouses, which has led to the dissolution of the marriage. The result is what some Christian leaders refer to as an irreparably "scrambled egg." What they mean is that the marital troubles and divorce decisions have gone so far that one or both spouses have lost the will to continue and have taken actions to lead a peaceable life without the marital relationship.

This booklet does not address the obvious: The spouses have missed God's good intentions for marital bliss. Instead, it focuses on recovering from divorce. The following suggestions are grounded in biblical teachings. They promote healing of damaged emotions and destructive behaviors through prayer and acceptance of the grace of Jesus Christ. And they include actions that can produce growth in Christian character and relationships. When these suggestions are heeded, a commitment to improve with the help of the Holy Spirit and a desire to walk in spiritual and relational health usually follow.

May you be blessed by this book. May you experience God's love as you read its pages and search for God's wisdom. Most of all, may you find all that God offers you as you recover from divorce.

But one thing I do: forgetting what
lies behind and reaching forward
to what lies ahead.
Philippians 3:13b

Scenes of Pain and Opportunity

Your Spouse Has Divorced You

Surprise? Shock? Relief? Sorrow? Anger? Confusion? Fear? Embarrassment? Shame? In a given day you could be experiencing any number of emotions and thoughts about being abandoned by your spouse.

Daydreams may fluctuate, ranging from visions of how to get revenge to visions of how to get restarted. Sometimes you may feel numb and incapable of entertaining any hopeful ideas about finding a way out of the mess.

Your worth as a spouse already has been seriously questioned, and your worth as a person may be next in line. Who are you *now*? Pause for a moment and think about something: How can you possibly recover from divorce and experience future loving relationships until you again feel acceptable and lovable as an individual? Did you know that God wants you to experience such acceptance and love through a deeply personal relationship with Him? Did you know that this experience is possible?

You still need the kind of intimate and significant relationship marriage offers. But now you feel ambivalent about forming new, trusting relationships. Living in your home, particularly during evenings and weekends, has become a different experience. You need security, comfort, and familiarity, but they seem to be on a long vacation.

Divorced persons are often tempted to get quickly involved in another intimate relationship to fill the emptiness left by the divorce. But it is important to remember that you may end up in another unhealthy and short-lived relationship if you're functioning out of emotional neediness rather than spiritual readiness. The result is double-heartache! Keep reading. The following information about healing and recovery can help you, just as it has helped others.

Ron's story is a common one. Ron was deeply depressed following his divorce. Even though he was beginning to understand his contributions to his wife's decision to leave the marriage, Ron's depression was still frequently expressed through intense anger. He would spend hours devising ways to get revenge. These vengeful thoughts would lead to outbursts of anger that were followed by days of withdrawal. Eventually, Ron married another woman, but he soon experienced similar problems that led to another divorce. The treatment team helped Ron understand what he was experiencing and inspired him to hope for a secure future. The team let him wrestle with his emotional pain as he got to know the Lord Jesus; then Ron experienced relief and began to make some healthy decisions based on faith and obedience. Finally, he and his team planned a year of recovery experiences founded on the Word of God. Ron recovered.

Months and even years of floundering can be prevented by planning a course of recovery and then sticking with the plan. This work is essential for your recovery.

You Have Divorced Your Spouse

Shame and subsequent dysfunctional relationships are two common recovery problems for persons who have divorced their spouses.

A person often makes the decision to divorce his or her spouse after several active attempts to improve the relationship (perhaps through prayer, counseling, and so forth) or after years of trying passively and unsuccessfully to communicate that the marriage is filled with a great deal of pain. Whatever has been tried has not worked, and one of the spouses decides to call it quits.

The resulting shame can become too painful to acknowledge, so the person may avoid discussing troubling thoughts and emotions with anyone. Instead, he or she may communicate the pain indirectly through highly destructive alcohol abuse, unsatisfying sexual relationships, workaholism, or withdrawal.

One of the most destructive actions a divorced spouse can take is to become involved in a new, often substitutionary, relationship before the recovery process has been completed. The divorce rate for second marriages is even higher than for first marriages. This statistic testifies to the fact that most divorced persons do not take the time to embark on a personal recovery journey engineered by God before they "try it all again." The results are usually disastrous.

5

You may be wondering why becoming intimately involved too soon in another relationship does not lead to healing and recovery. After all, this approach is successfully depicted in many movies and television programs! You know the story: Man leaves woman (or woman leaves man), falls in love with just the "right" person, and lives happily ever after (maybe even in another galaxy these days).

Healing and recovery are spiritual phenomena. This means your relationship with God must be healed before you can achieve lasting gains in any other arena, such as human relationships. A fast, substitutionary relationship will prevent you from keeping a clear mind about actions you need to take to be reconciled with God.

One of the first actions you must take to be reconciled with God is to allow yourself a time of grieving. Grief is simply experiencing truthful feelings about losses and shortcomings that have resulted in intense pain

6

for ourselves or others. Grieving allows us to move closer to God because it involves being honest or truthful. God is spirit and must be worshiped (approached) in spirit—and in truth. Gary Collins, a well-known Christian counselor and prolific writer, in his book, *Christian Counseling* (Dallas: Word Inc., Revised Edition, 1988), places a chapter on grief under the heading "Identity Issues." This is appropriate because grieving always involves a questioning of one's identity; thus, godly grieving always results in a reconciliation of one's identity with God. The result is a feeling of peace.

Grieving usually follows predictable stages: denial, anger, depression, bargaining, and acceptance. Effective grieving involves a highly individualized progression through each stage. Problems occur when a person becomes stuck in one stage and allows the emotional characteristics of that stage to dominate his or her life. The dynamics of these stages of grief are described more fully in the next chapter.

Another reason to avoid fast, substitutionary relationships in dealing with the pain of divorce is that you first need to discover what qualities you possess and what qualities you are attracted to that contribute to a dysfunctional marital relationship. Too often, a divorced person winds up becoming involved with someone who is just like the former spouse. When this discovery is realized, the "same old things" are usually tried to "fix" the spouse—without any good result. The outcome? Another defeated relationship. The solution to this destructive cycle is prevention. Keep in mind that divorce recovery is primarily a spiritual process. It involves allowing God to change your heart and ways *before* you risk reinjuring yourself or others in new relationships.

PERSONAL HEALING AND RECOVERY

Jesus Tells the Truth about Divorce

Jesus Christ had deeply truthful views about the dissolution of a marriage. His words about divorce are recorded in Matthew 5:31–32, Mark 10:2–12, and Luke 16:18. For persons recovering from divorce, two significant lessons can be learned from His teachings.

Jesus clearly taught that divorce is sinful when He identified its roots as hard-heartedness (Mark 10:5), its frequent catalyst as fornication (Matthew 5:32a), and its logical outcome as adultery (Luke 16:18). Adultery is forbidden by one of the Ten Commandments given to Moses by God on Mount Sinai (Exodus 20:14). Excusing this unrighteousness of divorce will not produce a forward step in your divorce recovery. We cannot ignore God's laws because they are written on our hearts (Romans 2:14–15); therefore, deep inside we know we have been disobedient. This disobedience produces negative consequences as we "reap" what we "sow" (Galatians 6:7–8).

But there is good news, too. Jesus' second lesson for persons recovering from divorce tells us hard-heartedness is changeable (Ephesians 4:22–24) and adultery is forgivable! We know this to be true because Jesus forgave adulterers and admonished them to stop committing adultery (John 8:10–11). Before you choose to remarry, or even if you are already remarried, I believe Jesus would have you stop right in your tracks, seek godly counsel, then read, understand, and apply the truth of the Scriptures to your life before you risk repeating marital troubles. The time to act is now.

The Lord is willing and able to forgive you because He paid for the price of your divorce with His own blood. Jesus is not asking you to repay Him through guilt, agony, fear, or self-inflicted injuries. He is asking you to learn from your mistakes, to be transformed by renewing your mind, and to walk in obedience and peace of mind. Jesus is not asking you to take revenge on your former spouse. He is asking you to do unto your former spouse as you would have him or her do unto you—in forgiveness.

Self-Worth and Recovery

Feelings and emotions are God-given barometers by which we measure how well we are. A variety of factors (such as physical health, poor performance, and rejection by a loved one) influence whether we feel good or bad about ourselves. The point is, no matter how we got there, we either feel good or bad about ourselves and we draw conclusions about our self-worth from these subjective feelings.

Now let us look at the impact of divorce on how you feel about yourself and on what you have concluded about your worth as a person. What has happened?

- You may feel you have *failed* because you did not remain married and faithful to your spouse.

- You may have experienced *disapproval* from your former spouse, children, relatives, and friends.

- As you have struggled with failure and disapproval, someone is probably paying for these feelings—you may be *punishing* either yourself or someone else for these "crimes."

12

• You may feel that not only what you have done is bad but that you are also a bad person, full of *shame*.

When a divorced person feels any of these painful emotions, there is a good probability he or she will respond very destructively. Some examples of destructive responses are:

1. Desiring to take one's own life
2. Desiring to take someone else's life
3. Being emotionally abusive to others
4. Being physically abusive to others
5. Developing appetite disturbances
6. Developing chronic depression
7. Having sexual intercourse outside of marriage
8. Taking impulsive actions (e.g., reckless speeding, quitting a job, kidnapping the children)
9. Becoming dependent on alcohol or drugs
10. Thinking "crazy" thoughts

To successfully deal with the normal and sometimes overwhelming emotions of divorce, a person must have assurance that he or she has remained in favor with God throughout the pain of failure, rejection, punishment, and shame. This undeserved favor, called *grace*, has been assured for every Christian. Paul described grace in his letter to the church in Rome: "For all have sinned and fall short of the glory of God, being justified as a gift by His grace through the redemption which is in Christ Jesus" (Romans 3:23–24).

God's love for and acceptance of you are unconditional. Your alertness and growing ability to walk in Jesus' redemption result in healing and recovery. Robert S. McGee's book, *The Search for Significance* (Rapha Publishing/Word, Inc.: Houston and Dallas, 2d ed., 1990), describes how you can learn to walk in Christ's redemption. The book describes four false beliefs that can trigger hopelessness and ineffective actions by a person seeking divorce healing. God's specific solutions to the four false beliefs also are given, along with the results you can expect from these solutions. They are as follows:

False Belief: *I must meet certain standards in order to feel good about myself.*
Consequences of False Belief: The fear of failure; perfectionism; being driven to succeed; manipulating others to achieve success; withdrawing from healthy risks
God's Specific Solution: *Because of* justification, *I am completely forgiven and fully pleasing to God. I no longer have to fear failure.*
Results of God's Specific Solution: Increasing freedom from the fear of failure; desire to pursue the right things: Christ and His kingdom; love for Christ

False Belief: *I must have the approval of certain others to feel good about myself.*

Consequences of False Belief: The fear of rejection; attempting to please others at any cost; being overly sensitive to criticism; withdrawing from others to avoid disapproval

God's Specific Solution: *Because of reconciliation, I am totally accepted by God. I no longer have to fear rejection.*

Results of God's Specific Solution: Increasing freedom from the fear of rejection; willingness to be open and vulnerable; able to relax around others; willingness to take criticism; desire to please God no matter what others think

False Belief: *Those who fail (including myself) are unworthy of love and deserve to be punished.*

Consequences of False Belief: The fear of punishment; propensity to punish others; blaming self and others for personal failure; withdrawing from God and fellow believers; being driven to avoid punishment

God's Specific Solution: *Because of* propitiation, *I am deeply loved by God. I no longer have to fear punishment or punish others.*

Results of God's Specific Solution: Increasing freedom from the fear of punishment; patience and kindness toward others; being quick to apply forgiveness; deep love for Christ

False Belief: *I am what I am. I cannot change. I am hopeless.*

Consequences of False Belief: Feelings of shame, hopelessness, inferiority; passivity; loss of creativity; isolation, withdrawing from others

God's Specific Solution: *Because of* regeneration, *I have been made brand new, complete in Christ. I no longer need to experience the pain of shame.*

Results of God's Specific Solution: Christ-centered self-confidence; joy, courage, peace; desire to know Christ

Continual study and application of these freeing, biblical truths will help you establish the cornerstone of a healthy self-concept in Christ. From this cornerstone you can develop all other recovery steps described in this book. Begin by reciting daily the following declaration, which gives life to the principles by focusing Christ's redeeming grace directly on you.

DECLARATION*

Because of Christ's redemption,
I am a new creation of infinite worth.

I am deeply loved,
I am completely forgiven,
I am fully pleasing,
I am totally accepted by God.
I am absolutely complete in Christ.

When my performance
reflects my new identity in Christ,
that reflection is dynamically unique.

There has never been another person like me
in the history of mankind,
nor will there ever be.
God has made me an original,
one of a kind, a special person.

* This excerpt from *The Search for Significance*
resource materials printed with permission from
Rapha, Inc.

King David and Divorce Recovery

The Bible story that best illustrates the essential ingredients of a recovery and restoration process is the story of David, Bathsheba, Uriah the Hittite, and Nathan the Prophet. This story is told in chapters 11 and 12 of 2 Samuel, and by David, himself, in Psalm 51. David saw Bathsheba, the wife of Uriah the Hittite, as she was bathing one evening. He was overcome by lust for her. Uriah, who was a member of David's army, was out of town on military duty. David sent his messengers to bring Bathsheba to him, and he had sexual intercourse with her. Bathsheba became pregnant, so David called Uriah back from battle on furlough. He hoped Uriah and Bathsheba would make love and Uriah would be fooled into believing that the unborn child was his. But Uriah made a vow of chastity in support of his army buddies! Next, David arranged for Uriah to be killed in battle, then he took Bathsheba to be his wife and she bore him a son.

Enter Nathan the prophet, who was appointed by God to be a spiritual mentor and personal advisor for David. Nathan cleverly confronted David with his sins and deceptions. David admitted his sins and accepted responsibility for their consequences. Then Nathan foretold two specific consequences: David's family would continually engage in a great deal of infighting and murderous schemes that would lead to several deaths; and the son from David and Bathsheba's affair would die (the child was then struck ill by the Lord and died seven days later). Both predictions came true, producing considerable heartbreak for David for the rest of his life. However, David did recover! He even wrote a song, called Psalm 51, which describes his prayer to God during the recovery process. God's response to David will be examined in just a moment. First, read and reflect on Psalm 51.

Psalm 51, (NIV)

Have mercy on me, O God,
　　according to your unfailing love;
according to your great compassion
　　blot out my transgressions.
Wash away all my iniquity
　　and cleanse me from my sin.

For I know my transgressions,
　　and my sin is always before me.
Against you, you only, have I sinned
　　and done what is evil in your sight,
so that you are proved right when you
　　　　speak
　　and justified when you judge.
Surely I was sinful at birth,
　　sinful from the time my mother
　　　　conceived me.

Surely you desire truth in the inner
　　　　parts;
　　you teach me wisdom in the inmost
　　　　place.

Cleanse me with hyssop, and I will be
   clean;
      wash me, and I will be whiter than
      snow.
Let me hear joy and gladness;
   let the bones you have crushed
   rejoice.
Hide your face from my sins
   and blot out all my iniquity.

Create in me a pure heart, O God,
   and renew a steadfast spirit within
   me.
Do not cast me from your presence
   or take your Holy Spirit from me.
Restore to me the joy of your salvation
   and grant me a willing spirit, to
   sustain me.

Then I will teach transgressors your
   ways,
   and sinners will turn back to you.

Save me from bloodguilt, O God,
 the God who saves me,
  and my tongue will sing of your
   righteousness.
O Lord, open my lips,
  and my mouth will declare your
   praise.
You do not delight in sacrifice, or I
   would bring it;
  you do not take pleasure in burnt
   offerings.
The sacrifices of God are a broken
    spirit;
  a broken and contrite heart,
  O God, you will not despise.

In your good pleasure make Zion
    prosper;
  build up the walls of Jerusalem.
Then there will be righteous sacrifices,
  whole burnt offerings to delight
    you;
  then bulls will be offered on your
   altar.

Right away you can see that David's words were primarily confessions of sinfulness and prayers for forgiveness. A closer examination of Psalm 51 reveals several key steps that apply to divorce recovery, as well as to any recovery and restoration process.

1. David felt and expressed his sorrow: "The sacrifices of God are a broken spirit; / a broken and contrite heart, / O God, you will not despise."

2. David confessed the truth about his sinfulness: "For I know my transgressions, / and my sin is always before me. / Against you, you only, have I sinned / and done what is evil in your sight."

3. David respected God's justice: "...so that you are proved right when you speak / and justified when you judge."

4. David found refreshment in God's love for him as a person even though his ac-

tions had been sinful: "Have mercy on me, O God, / according to your unfailing love; / according to your great compassion / blot out my transgressions."

5. David sought forgiveness and renewal from God: "Wash away all my iniquity / and cleanse me from my sin... / Cleanse me with hyssop, and I will be clean; / wash me and I will be whiter than snow / Create in me a pure heart, O God, / and renew a steadfast spirit within me. / Do not cast me from your presence or take your Holy Spirit from me. / Restore to me the joy of your salvation / and grant me a willing spirit, to sustain me."

6. David chose to act on his faith in God's redeeming power: "Then I will teach transgressors your ways, / and sinners will turn back to you. / Save me from bloodguilt, O God, / the God who saves me, / and my tongue will sing of your righteousness. / O Lord, open my lips, / and my mouth will declare your praise."

7. David desired that his actions would not hinder other people from honoring God or from maturing in their relationship with God: "In your good pleasure make Zion prosper, / build up the walls of Jerusalem. / Then there will be righteous sacrifices, / whole burnt offerings to delight you, / then bulls will be offered on your altar."

Did God forgive and restore David? The answer lies in the rest of this story and in two books that were written after David's death. After the death of David and Bathsheba's child conceived out of wedlock, another child was born to them. They named him Solomon. When David died, Solomon became the king of Israel. Chapter 3 of 1 Kings tells how Solomon was visited by the Lord in a dream. This was the same Lord, remember, to whom David had confessed his sins and had asked for forgiveness and restoration. Solomon said to God, "Thou hast shown great lovingkindness to Thy servant David my father, according as he walked before Thee in truth and righteousness and uprightness of heart toward Thee; and Thou hast reserved for him this great lovingkindness, that Thou hast given him a son to sit on his throne as it is this day" (1 Kings 3:6).

David? Faithful to God and upright in heart? Just think how a merciless and unforgiving God might have answered Solomon: "Who are you kidding? Your old man blew his opportunity to be faithful and upright to me. Dream on!"

Instead, this is how our loving God responded to Solomon: "And if you walk in My ways, keeping My statutes and commandments, as your father David walked, then I will prolong your days" (1 Kings 3:14).

The second text that confirms God's forgiveness and restoration of David is in the New Testament: "The book of the genealogy of Jesus Christ, the son of David, the son of Abraham.... And to David was born Solomon

by her who had been the wife of Uriah..."
(Matthew 1:1, 6).

The first chapter of the first book of the
New Testament remains as a testimony of
the power and desire of God to forgive us
and to make our crooked paths straight. Did
God forgive and restore David? Absolutely.
Incredible? Not if you seek and find recovery
the way David did. I have experienced God's
mercy, love, and forgiveness in my own
divorce recovery. You can, too!

GRIEVING: HURT, ANGER, AND FORGIVENESS

Then Peter came and said to Him,
"Lord, how often shall my brother sin
against me and I forgive him?
Up to seven times?"
Jesus said to him, "I do not say to
you, up to seven times, but up to
seventy times seven.

Matthew 18:21–22

Perhaps you are having great difficulty finding peace in your heart. You may be trapped in a vicious cycle of hurt, anger, and unforgiveness toward your former spouse.

Symptoms of this trap often include depression that will not lift, mood swings, and continual blaming of others for your condition. God wants you to experience relief from these lingering symptoms. He wants you to escape from your trap.

A necessary part of divorce recovery is fully experiencing the grief associated with the marriage failure. As we mentioned earlier, the most frequent stages of grief are denial, anger, depression, bargaining, and acceptance. In our treatment centers many persons are counseled who have remained stuck in denial (emotional numbness) following their divorce. Numbness can be a pretty good initial response to intense emotional pain because it allows our brains to sort out the information at a pace we can handle. This numbness often gives rise to anger at our inability to get our needs met. Anger is also a valid feeling and must be experienced from time to time. But to be overwhelmed by extended anger often leads to bitterness that only exacerbates a problem and alienates people. If you are still easily influenced by feelings of anger about your divorce, it may be time to allow yourself to feel sorrow.

Feeling sorrow is essential to discovering the nature and extent of your woundedness and to experiencing the acceptance, forgiveness, and love of Jesus Christ. The Bible describes two types of sorrow: worldly and godly (2 Corinthians 7:10). Worldly sorrow is an expression of hopelessness that can lead to death. Occasionally your sorrow may be so overwhelming that you experience thoughts of suicide or homicide. If you have these thoughts, I encourage you to telephone a friend, a pastor, or a professional counselor and get the help you need. You are experiencing a form of sorrow that is outside of God's intentions for your recovery. Godly sorrow, on the other hand, leads to repentance from self-deceptions and unhealthy actions.

And this repentance, in turn, leads you to discover your need for Christ and affirms your worth as a person in Him.

This may be hard for you to swallow right now, but the bondage of unforgiveness will choke the life out of you with the rope of bitterness. You need to forgive your former spouse *today*. This does not mean you have to trust your former spouse or concede that what has been done to you is okay. In fact, it would be unscriptural for you to simply excuse offensive behaviors or to trust someone who has offended you and has not reconciled with you (Matthew 18:15–17). You are held in bondage, however, by choosing not to forgive your former spouse. Read Jesus' words about forgiveness in Matthew 18:21–35. You will see how unforgiveness brings physical, emotional, and spiritual torment. In contrast, forgiveness is a commandment that holds a promise of peace.

A professional counselor once had a client who became irate when the counselor suggested that one reason he had married was to have someone to blame for his own failures. Similarly, the client's divorce gave him something to blame for his adamant deceptions about successful relationships. Unfortunately, this man never returned for more counseling. Are *you* ready to stop blaming someone or something else and humbly ask God to uncover the source of your bitterness and deception?

Surrender and Acceptance

> *Come to Me, all who are weary and heavy-laden, and I will give you rest. Take My yoke upon you, and learn from Me, for I am gentle and humble in heart; and you shall find rest for your souls. For My yoke is easy, and My load is light."*
>
> Matthew 11:28–30

Many years of counseling troubled people have led me to conclude there are two basic types who resist recovery. One type is easily stuck in the mud of life's failures and would rather focus on the mud than on getting out of it. The second type consists of people who are always running through the mud as fast as possible, splashing mud on themselves and others, and denying that the puddles are muddy at all.

People who surrender to Jesus and learn from Him will soon become discontented with being stuck in the mud or with splashing mud everywhere. Some will speed up and others will slow down to meet Jesus on the road to recovery.

Later, we will examine how certain relationships can stand in the way of your recovery. However, when experienced under the easy yoke of Jesus Christ, some of these relationships can become a source of comfort and stability; even relationships that have to change following a divorce can become sources of personal growth. But first comes your relationship with God. I do not believe anyone can recover from divorce until his or her self-worth is derived from a solid relationship with God and is clearly separated and set above any self-worth derived from relationships with people. If you are waiting for another person to fill the vacuum in your soul and make you ready to surrender to God, then you will wait forever. It is simply not God's plan to sustain us through anyone other than Himself; human relationships are His way of enriching us, not sustaining us.

Read the first of the Ten Commandments: "You shall have no other gods before Me" (Exodus 20:3). Having no other gods before the Father, the Son, and the Holy Spirit means more than not praying to an idol! For a person recovering from divorce, it means giving up anyone or anything else that is the basis of your worth and significance.

For some people, surrender means giving up deep emotional pain. Search first to see whether you may be secretly deriving some benefit from staying in the pain. For example, it might allow you to continue avoiding relationships, or keep you blaming others instead of taking responsibility for your actions. Then you must make a conscious decision to release the pain through forgiveness of certain persons. As you give up the pain, replace it with God's love and acceptance.

If you are more deeply troubled, surrender may involve giving up addictive relationships or substances that are keeping you from feeling legitimate painful emotions (for example, drowning your sorrows in alcohol or obsessive shopping). Then, as you work through your sorrow and anger and choose to forgive and to accept forgiveness, you will begin to experience God's love and acceptance.

You may even be in deeper trouble because you have *never* experienced God's love and acceptance. Or perhaps you have placed God on probation, with certain terms to be fulfilled before you will allow Him to help you. In our treatment centers many people who do not understand God's love and forgiveness have set conditions for emotional healing that God is not willing to meet. For instance, they might first insist on understanding why their divorce happened, or demand that God heal them immediately, or require God to take revenge. Some of these persons have benefited from a truly Christian therapeutic relationship with someone who has earned their trust and has let them experience Jesus' love as it has been manifested through one of His followers. Others have been motivated to consider God's love and acceptance due to a lack of other viable alternatives. After all, salvation by grace, rather than works, is a uniquely Christian concept. And it has redeeming power because it is God's truth. Surrendering to God and recognizing His acceptance of you and others is an essential part of divorce recovery. May God restore you to health as you apply His truths to your life!

Divorce Recovery and Professional Counseling

Many persons who are earnestly trying to recover from divorce sometimes find themselves unable to move forward. Often, being stuck is related to their lack of objectivity about themselves and their relationships. Professional counseling from a clinically competent, Christian therapist can help. Ask your doctor, minister, or someone else you trust to recommend a suitable counselor. Set up an initial appointment to describe your situation to the counselor and to evaluate your compatibility with him or her. Do not hesitate to change counselors if you feel incompatible or if a treatment technique is out of line with your Christian values.

Primary Relationships

Everyone needs affirmation, the feeling that another person has recognized our worthiness of his or her love and acceptance. Divorce interrupts a common source of affirmation. It is as though a vital flow of water has been turned off; the divorced person begins rapidly to thirst for affirmation. This thirst can cause an imbalance in all primary relationships as the person seeks to reestablish the flow of affirmation. These relationships will be the focus of this section. Common problems will be addressed and practical advice will be provided.

Former Spouse

No matter how troubled the marriage may have been, when two people are married, they "become one flesh" (Genesis 2:24). Severing flesh hurts. It takes time to adapt to losing a spouse. We miss the relationship, even if we are the ones who initiated the divorce. The spouse who was divorced probably feels even worse.

Kay talked openly about how she was able to relate caringly and clearly to her former husband, Larry. Kay already had an advantage many divorced persons do not have: she was willing and able to separate what she was responsible for versus what Larry was responsible for. She accepted responsibility for her actions but did not accept responsibility for Larry's actions; nor did she feel compelled to "fix" Larry. Here is Kay's advice for relating to a former spouse:

1. Stop the "blame game." Faultfinding is emotionally draining, seldom satisfying, and never healing.

2. Seek reconciliation of the relationship or acceptance of the divorce through counseling. As soon as possible, stop the wishy-washiness and plot a course of recovery through clear goals and pure motives.

3. Make a commitment to work together for the children's sake. When you discern that you or the former spouse is manipulating the children, knock it off.

4. Do not manipulate the former spouse. One common form of manipulation is to hold out hope for reconciliation (when you have no intentions of reconciling) to motivate your former spouse to go along with you or to leave you alone. Another frequent manipulation is to inspire guilt!

5. Read Matthew 18:21–35 about the importance of forgiveness. Remember that forgiving and trusting are not the same. You can choose to cancel a debt without becoming a doormat for the debtor.

6. Do not be overwhelmed or controlled by your feelings about your former spouse.

7. Pray for the former spouse. Do not pray manipulatively to instruct God how to do *your* will. Rather, turn the former spouse over to God for conviction and for correction in all matters. Pray that God would reveal His will for the life of your former spouse.

8. Live your own life. Make whatever changes are possible to establish your own routines.

The Children

Even in the most gracious divorce, nothing can hurt more than watching your children experience the pain when God's plan for nurturing them turns sour. Deep concern for children of divorce is definitely warranted. Studies indicate these children can be vulnerable to physical, emotional, intellectual, and spiritual difficulties.

Let us examine child-rearing from the point of view of Sam and Pam who struggled with the issue a great deal but who succeeded in creating a loving and harmonious environment for their children.

Pam's Story

Pam has been divorced for two years. Sam, her former husband, has remarried, but Pam has not. Pam has custody of Billy, 12, and Shelly, 10. Pam became a Christian four years ago. When Pam's former husband divorced her, she was understandably distraught. She immediately sought help from her pastor, who referred her to a professionally trained Christian counselor. Pam remained in counseling for five months after the divorce. She recounts the advice she received and implemented under the guidance of her pastor and counselor:

> They told me my children's recovery from the divorce would be directly proportional to my own commitment to recover by remaining accountable to a few stable, wise,

and godly people. I made up my mind that, no matter how I felt, I would allow these trusted care-givers to get close to me and my children. I decided I would try what they asked me to try. My ability to stabilize my family was the result of several steps I took in response to their advice during counseling:

1. I strengthened my own foundation of hope and obedience by embarking on a personal journey in the light of the Lord and the power of His might.
2. I raised my children to relate to God the Father as He was revealed by Jesus Christ through prayer and through biblical truths.
3. I explained that my former husband and I were responsible

for missing the mark of God's plan for our family. I stressed to the children that they were blameless.

4. I established consistency and a positive attitude about the children's safe visits with their father. I did not withhold them from him in order to express my anger toward him.

5. I made sure that the home, school, and church environments for my children were physically and emotionally safe. They could say what they were feeling and those feelings were respected, even though we often could not change the situation.

6. I established a loving discipline plan and implemented the plan as consistently as I could. It wasn't perfect, but the children knew what behaviors were

unacceptable. They also knew that disobedience would result in logical consequences that were given in love.

7. I tried to establish a consistent daily living arrangement so that the children would know what each day's routine would be. I often had to rely on baby-sitters and late dinners, but the children usually knew what the plan was and they knew they would be treated properly. I made sure that the time we spent together was "quality time" focused on our family. I developed the attitude that an hour together with my children is more important than vacuuming.

8. After our lives were reestablished, I went to a seminar series at our church about the developmental stages of

children's growth. Both of my children are almost adolescents. I learned how each year becomes connective tissue for the next year. So if certain connections are poorly developed, the child can stay stuck at that stage until certain needs are met. Through relations with his father and other positive role models my son is learning how to become a healthy adult without a father in the house. My daughter is also learning basic attitudes and skills to prepare her for the roles of wife, mother, and employee. We talk openly about those realities and encourage each other in the Lord.

Sam's Story

Sam has been remarried for two years. His dilemma has been how to cope with the loss of daily contact with his children, Billy and Shelly, and how to provide for them in his new role as an "absent father." Sam also received professional counseling and shares his advice to other men in a similar situation.

I did not fully understand it then, but now I know that my primary struggles as a divorced father were with guilt and hopelessness. I felt guilty because I had failed to "be there" for my children after the divorce. I felt hopeless because I wasn't sure I really *could* be "there." I didn't know if I could have a mutually affirming relationship with my children. Now I feel hopeful, probably because I have experienced many satisfying moments with them. I love them and they know it. They love me and I know it. It is working. Let me tell you what I did:

1. I had to learn first that even
   though I felt I had "failed" as a
   husband, I was not a failure as a
   human being in the eyes of a
   loving and merciful God. God
   loves and accepts me, and He
   has forgiven me.

2. I recognized that even though
   my own father had been present
   in our home, he was emotionally
   absent from my life. He did not
   tell me he loved me and he
   expected me to be "perfect" in
   all my endeavors. I resolved that
   even though I am physically
   absent from my children, when
   I do have them with me I will
   be very emotionally present. I
   tell them I love them. I hug them.
   I tell them it's okay to feel
   emotions—about the divorce or
   about anything. I laugh with

them when I feel happy and sometimes I cry when I feel sad. The quality of our time together is rich. Of course, I feel sad when they have to leave. But I feel a peace in knowing that I am beginning to love them more as God loves me.

3. I go to a Christian support group for divorced fathers. It has helped me understand and express my painful emotions. The most rewarding part has been our study of the characteristics of our heavenly Father. I've learned that God wants me to bless my children as He blesses me.

4. I do not blame my former spouse for the divorce and have forgiven her for any past offenses.

5. I maintain a consistent routine and a set of rules when the

children visit. This helps them adapt more easily in the transition from one home to the other. It also makes my former spouse's job easier as a single parent. When she and I both are happy, we are able to love the children better.

From these accounts, we learn that families torn by divorce have to contend with different issues than intact families have. The divorced family is no longer naturally constructed to provide as safe and complete a learning environment for the children. Be encouraged, however, that your children can receive a rich blessing from you if you are willing to take the recovery steps Pam and Sam took.

The Family of Origin

Divorce can generate a sense of failure and a fear of punishment when you talk to your own parents about the divorce. You may find yourself responding as you did when you were a child.

If you were reared by parents who fostered a great deal of emotional dependence on them, you will find that a part of you is preparing for their possible rejection of you. This can make you feel very uncomfortable and ashamed when you discuss the divorce with them. They may respond with anger or despair, as though the divorce reflected their failure as parents. Either reaction may make the divorce twice as difficult for you because your parents are responding as though you are an extension of them.

Even if you were reared by parents who fostered a great deal of independence, you may still find yourself uncomfortable talking with them about your divorce. Fear of failure, rejection, and punishment can influence these interactions. If you and your family are uncomfortable expressing emotions, you may downplay the pain you are feeling, joke about your situation, or even not talk about it at all, pretending that it really did not happen.

Alan announced the news of his divorce to his parents one spring evening as they were sitting in the den reading the newspaper and watching television. Alan's family has always had difficulty expressing emotional warmth to one another, so Alan's announcement was objective as he had been trained to communicate such news. Alan's parents did not move, did not blink, and did not betray their feelings with even the remotest reaction. When Alan had finished, his mother said, "I knew the marriage would never work." Alan's heart sank as he choked back tears. What he needed to hear was love, support, and acceptance. What he heard instead was, *It's no surprise that you didn't meet our expectations for success*. He got a controlling response rather than the loving response he needed. It was no different than Alan's childhood experiences.

Because these dynamics of failure, rejection, blame, and shame do exist within many families, it will be important for you to plan your words about the divorce when you tell your parents. The following examples offer suggestions for addressing some common reactions.

Failure: "I feel as badly as you do that the marriage did not survive. However, I hope we can avoid viewing anyone as a 'failure.' We did our best, but it did not work."

Rejection: "Even though being married is no longer acceptable for either of us, I still accept my former spouse as a person. I hope you can continue to accept each of us, too."

Blame: "It would be too simple to single out any person or any issue as the cause of the divorce. We both share responsibility for the marriage not working. It would be really helpful right now for you not to blame anyone. We all need your support. Your grandchildren need to experience as little tension as possible. Could you help us by respecting our individual needs for your support and objectivity right now?"

Shame: "I suspect you may be feeling that our divorce reflects poorly on you as parents. We accept full responsibility for the divorce. It is not your fault. We may need to discuss any discomfort you expect to have in sharing this news with your friends or our relatives. Maybe I can offer suggestions about how to handle these conversations."

The goal is for you to be as honest as you need to be with your parents about the divorce and how it is affecting everyone. By sharing your needs and concerns you will give your parents the opportunity to accept a helping role.

Your divorce could be the first family crisis that anyone has attempted to really talk about together. It can be a special time of getting closer as a family.

If, after prayer and rehearsal, your parents do not respond with support and care, it may be necessary to seek help and support from friends, siblings, your minister, or a professional counselor. Plan with them how to effectively respond to your parents' attitude and behaviors regarding the divorce.

The Church

Within any community of Christians, an obligation exists to exhort the members to be obedient to God's laws and to remain accountable to God for all actions. Methods to discourage sin and to encourage growth in Christian character will vary from church to church. The goal is to ensure that the person who disobeys God's law has the best opportunity for conviction, repentance, correction, and restoration of fellowship with the body of Christ. Then, as Paul suggests in 2 Corinthians 2:5–11, Christians should forgive and reaffirm love for the sinner. It is entirely possible that your church has the fullness of ministries to rightfully confront disobedient actions in this way and then to lovingly and graciously affirm the person. I urge you not to make a hasty decision to dissociate with the church based on emotional pain you may experience during a disciplinary process. On the other hand, I could not encourage you to remain in a church in which you do not experience God's love and acceptance from the members following a divorce decision.

If your church has support groups, go to them. By having such assistance programs, your church is directly telling you that the leadership supports honesty about painful aspects of living and wants to help you recover within the body of Christ.

Your New Spouse

Divorce recovery seldom ends at the point remarriage begins. If, before remarrying, you have drawn closer to God, examined your own shortcomings, and matured through studying and applying God's Word, you may be well on the way to experiencing a happy marriage with your new spouse. Perhaps it has taken the wisdom, perseverance, and help of counselors to encourage such growth.

If you are considering remarriage or have already remarried but are continuing to experience disharmony, it is not too late to make a commitment to recovery. Let's look at ways this can happen.

One common problem in the new marital relationship is feeling uncomfortable or threatened by your new spouse's relationship with his or her former spouse. It will be important for you to acknowledge together that the past relationship *was* significant. Now a different but continuing relationship may be necessary to conduct business or to nurture the children from the previous marriage. If you are experiencing difficulties as a couple regarding the relationship with the former spouse, and if these difficulties are intense or frequent, it will be essential for both of you to join a recovery support group. Individual counseling may be needed also.

The importance of providing love and discipline for the children of a divorced home cannot be stressed enough. Your new spouse may see your attempts to provide for your children as detracting from your efforts to detach from the past and solidify a new start. It is important to assure your new spouse that you share his or her desire for a new start and that you're eager to establish new traditions and goals as a married couple. This attitude can help the children accept the new stepparent's role. At the same time, it is important to affirm the welfare of the children. Discuss with your new spouse how each of you can contribute to the well-being of both the children and the new marriage. Again, if you are finding it difficult to work through these issues together, seek the advice of a good Christian counselor.

Differences in philosophies and methods of child discipline can play havoc with the stability of the new marriage. Thus, before remarriage both spouses are wise to participate in premarital counseling and parenting classes. The purpose of these programs is to encourage you to deal honestly with sticky issues and to reach agreement about them before the normal stresses of marital adjustment occur.

The Stepfamily

The most common cause of second divorces is the inability to establish a stepfamily that is committed to family-style communications, and committed to earning trust, being honest, accepting responsibility for choices, appreciating each other, and adjusting to the realities of stepfamily life.

In their book, *Strengthening Your Stepfamily* (Circle Pines, MN: American Guidance Service, 1986) Elizabeth Einstein and Linda Albert describe five stages in the development of a stepfamily: fantasy, confusion, crazy time, stability, and commitment. Families that do not make it through the first three stages do not make it—period!

The fantasy stage is characterized by unrealistic expectations that the positive aspects of the remarriage will always overshadow any problems that may arise. Sometimes this stage includes outright denial that any significant problems could ever occur. Feelings of "love" obscure deeper insights into the emotional and practical realities of stepfamily life.

The confusion stage results when the dynamics of the fantasy stage are reversed. The realities of painful emotions and maladjustments within the stepfamily begin to overshadow the initial feelings of love and harmony. It is a little like being hit unaware in the back of the head with a baseball. The dazed response is, "What the heck happened?"

Crazy time occurs when each member of the stepfamily reacts to the confusion stage by being a selfish individual instead of a team player. Each person's focus becomes, *My needs are not getting met and my needs are more important than anyone else's or than the integrity of the stepfamily*. The behaviors that result are isolation, anger, mistrust, defiance, blaming, and other destructive actions. These responses are all smoke screens for each member's obvious feelings of hurt and disappointment.

Fantasy, confusion, and crazy time were described by Bill, who once told his counselor, "When I remarried, I knew there would be some difficulties blending the children from our previous marriages, but I figured we could work out the rough spots in about six months to a year. After all, my wife and I are both Christians, we have a lot of love to give, and we are reasonable people. When we entered our third year and were still continually fighting about the same old issues, I knew we needed some major help. Thank God we decided to swallow our pride and get into counseling."

Stability happens as the husband and wife accept and model realistic expectations and become honest about their feelings of hurt or their fear about family losses. They begin to utilize the strengths of each family member to build a commitment to the stepfamily team. Then as the stepfamily becomes more realistic about expectations and allows true feelings to be expressed, it can begin to establish what it can and cannot do to meet each member's emotional needs. Such honesty develops trust and responsibility and moves the family into the commitment stage.

Commitment occurs when the stepfamily's members begin to enjoy being a part of the team. Enjoyment comes from giving and receiving love and support within the context of realistic expectations. For the first time, each person's past is respected. That means everyone acknowledges that stepfamily members came from different family configurations and it is okay to have significant, positive identification with parents or children who are not living within the stepfamily. The success of the stepfamily is built on a commitment to resolve "present-tense" issues within the bounds of the stepfamily. For example, if someone's feelings get hurt, the persons involved respect and trust each other enough to talk through the problem, get it worked out, and then move on. At this stage, minimal interference occurs from unresolved frustrations about relationship losses. The stepfamily takes care of its own business (emotions, decisions, etc.) with healthy, direct, caring communication. Problems no longer result in angry outbursts; they are no longer pushed underground, creating withdrawal and bitterness. Matters get put on the table "in truth and in love."

Because starting a stepfamily is complex and unnatural and because a God-given need exists for security and nurturance within a family, the stepfamily can become a stewpot for trouble. Do not hesitate to read together helpful books about stepfamily adjustment, such as *Strengthening Your Stepfamily*. Seek the advice and support of counselors who are familiar with the dynamics of stepfamilies or who have gone through similar experiences, themselves.

CONCLUSION

This book's purpose has been to encourage you to take several steps forward in the journey toward divorce healing and recovery. Let's take another quick look at that journey as we conclude our time together. As Christians, we know our relationships with Jesus Christ provide the way to overcome any difficulties. Yet divorce creates a heartfelt struggle to maintain our balance in the face of intense emotional pain and questioning of our worth as individuals. After divorce, we are prone to respond to our pain through actions that emotionally injure us or those persons we really desire to get close to.

Getting in touch with these painful emotions about your losses and working toward forgiveness and acceptance of situations you cannot change are steps in the grieving process. Divorced persons move toward forgiveness and acceptance as they become aware of how much God loves, accepts, and forgives them and their former spouses. His grace abounds!

Throughout the grieving process some relationships will be supportive while others may be stressful. While you may feel the need to become involved in an intimate relationship with the opposite sex soon after your divorce, it's important that you postpone this kind of action until the grieving process is in its final stages. The importance of acting responsibly, of keeping yourself and your children safe, and of effective communications has been emphasized throughout this booklet.

May God surround you with caring people who know how to listen to your heart and guide you through the volatile times. God will never give up on you. His mercy and wisdom will lift you up and set you on the road to recovery!

Editor's note

At Rapha, we believe that small groups can provide a nurturing and powerful environment to help people deal with real-life problems such as depression, grief, fear, eating disorders, chemical dependency, codependency, and all kinds of other relational and emotional difficulties. The warmth, honesty, and understanding in those groups helps us understand why we feel and act the way we do. And with the encouragement of others, we can take definitive steps toward healing and health for ourselves and our relationships.

Not all groups, however, provide this kind of "greenhouse" for growth. Some only perpetuate the guilt and loneliness by giving quick and superficial solutions to the deep and often complex problems in our lives.

We urge you to find a group of people in your church, or in a church near you, where the members provide acceptance, love, honesty, and encouragement. Rapha has many different books, workbooks, leader's guides, and types of training so that people in these groups can be nurtured in the love and grace of God and focused on sound biblical principles to help them experience healing and growth.

To obtain a free list of the materials we have available, please write to us at:

Rapha, Inc.
8876 Gulf Freeway, Suite 340
Houston, TX 77017

ABOUT THE AUTHOR...

David A. Smart, CSW-ACP is Rapha's Western Regional Director. He also speaks at their conferences and seminars. David received his Master of Arts in Psychology from the University of Nebraska.

Having experienced the heartache and stress of a divorce, himself, David's insight on the subjects of divorce recovery and stepfamilies stems from his own experience, as well as his clinical expertise. He and his wife, Linda, live in Scottsdale, Arizona with their two sons, Jeremy and Aaron.